Little Bakers, Big Flavors

Fun, Easy & Unique Desserts for Young Chefs

Alisha Kapani

Copyright © 2023 [Alisha Kapani]. All rights reserved.

The content contained within this book may not be reproduced, duplicated, or transmitted without direct written permission from the author or the publisher.

Under no circumstances will any blame or legal responsibility be held against the publisher, or author, for any damages, reparation, or monetary loss due to the information contained within this book, either directly or indirectly.

Legal Notice:
This book is copyright protected. It is only for personal use. You cannot amend, distribute, sell, use, quote, or paraphrase any part, or the content within this book, without the consent of the author or publisher.

Disclaimer Notice:
Please note the information contained within this document is for educational and entertainment purposes only. All effort has been executed to present accurate, up to date, reliable, complete information. No warranties of any kind are declared or implied. Readers acknowledge that the author is not engaged in the rendering of legal, financial, medical, or professional advice. The content within this book has been derived from various sources. Please consult a licensed professional before attempting any techniques outlined in this book.

By reading this document, the reader agrees that under no circumstances is the author responsible for any losses, direct or indirect, that are incurred as a result of the use of the information contained within this document, including, but not limited to, errors, omissions, or inaccuracies.

Table of Contents

Introduction..1
Rainbow Fruit Skewers...3
No-Bake Oreo Truffles...4
Fruit Pizza..5
Chocolate-Dipped Pretzel Rods..6
Banana Sushi...7
Apple Nachos..8
Frozen Yogurt Bark..9
Peanut Butter Energy Bites...10
Jelly Bean Bark...11
Mini Cheesecake Cups...12
Ice Cream Sandwiches...13
Fruity Frozen Popsicles..14
Caramel Popcorn..15
Colourful Yogurt Parfait..16
Graham Cracker Houses..17
Chocolate Banana Bites...18
Marshmallow Rice Krispies..19
Fruit Sorbet...20
Muddy Buddies..21
Chocolate-Covered Strawberries..22
Cinnamon Sugar Tortilla Crisps...23
Mini Fruit Tarts..24
Candy-Coated Pretzel Rods..25
Frozen Banana Pops...26
Berry Smoothie Bowls...27
Conclusion...28

Introduction

Welcome to "Little Bakers, Big Flavors: Fun, Easy & Unique Desserts for Young Chefs!" This cookbook is a celebration of the delightful world of desserts and the young culinary artists who bring their creative flair to the kitchen. Within these pages, budding chefs will embark on a flavorful journey, discovering an array of sweet treats that are not only scrumptious but also simple and enjoyable to prepare.

The Joy of Baking with Young Chefs
Cooking is an art, and for our young chefs, the kitchen is their canvas. This cookbook is designed to ignite their passion for baking, allowing them to explore the magic of creating delectable desserts. Here, they'll find recipes tailored to their skills, empowering them to take charge and whip up delightful confections that are as fun to make as they are to eat.

A Culinary Adventure Awaits
From ice-cream sandwiches to fruity popsicles, from rice krispies to creamy parfaits, "Little Bakers, Big Flavors" offers a diverse array of recipes, each promising an exciting culinary adventure. With step-by-step instructions young chefs will navigate through the recipes with ease, fostering confidence and fostering a sense of accomplishment with each delicious creation.

Embracing Creativity in the Kitchen

Cooking is an avenue for creativity, and this cookbook encourages our young chefs to unleash their imagination. They'll discover that the kitchen is their playground, where they can experiment with flavors, textures, and decorations to craft desserts that are not only tasty but uniquely their own. Whether it's adding a sprinkle of colorful toppings or inventing their signature twist to a classic recipe, the possibilities are endless.

Making Memories One Recipe at a Time

Beyond the delectable desserts, this cookbook is about the joy of cooking together. It's about cherishing the laughter, the flour-dusted high-fives, and the shared moments that transform simple ingredients into cherished memories. Through these recipes, families and friends will bond, sharing stories, and savoring the fruits of their collaborative kitchen endeavors.

Empowering Young Chefs

Cooking is a life skill, and "Little Bakers, Big Flavors" empowers our young chefs to embrace the kitchen confidently. By learning foundational baking techniques and understanding the joy of creating something from scratch, they'll develop a lifelong love for culinary exploration.

A Sweet Conclusion

In this cookbook, every recipe is a chapter waiting to be explored, a delightful story waiting to unfold. "Little Bakers, Big Flavors" is more than a collection of recipes; it's an invitation to embark on a flavorful journey, to create lasting memories, and to celebrate the joys of baking. So grab your aprons, gather your ingredients, and let's bake our way to a world of sweet adventures together!

Rainbow Fruit Skewers

Serves: 6 skewers   Prep time: 20 min   Cook time: 0 min

INGREDIENTS

Strawberries (red)

Mandarin oranges (orange)

Pineapple chunks (yellow)

Green grapes (green)

Blueberries (blue)

Purple grapes (indigo)

Raspberries (violet)

Wooden skewers

DIRECTIONS

1. Wash the fruits nicely.
2. Cut the strawberries in half.
3. Peel the oranges and break them into pieces.
4. Chop the pineapple into small squares.
5. Wash the grapes.
6. Arrange the fruits in this order: red (strawberries), orange (mandarin oranges), yellow (pineapple), green (grapes), blue (blueberries), indigo (purple grapes), violet (raspberries).
7. Slide the fruits onto the wooden skewers in the rainbow order. Start with a strawberry half, then an orange piece, pineapple square, grapes, blueberries, purple grapes, and finally, a raspberry.
8. Put the rainbow fruit skewers on a plate or serve them directly.

No-Bake Oreo Truffles

Serves: 20 truffles   Prep time: 30 min   Cook time: 0 min

INGREDIENTS

1 package of Oreo cookies

4 ounces of cream cheese, softened

1 cup of chocolate chips (milk or dark)

Sprinkles (optional)

DIRECTIONS

1. Crush the Oreos:
   - Put the Oreo cookies into a sealable plastic bag.
   - Use a rolling pin or the back of a spoon to crush the cookies until they become fine crumbs.
2. Mix Cookies and Cream Cheese:
   - In a mixing bowl, combine the crushed Oreos with the softened cream cheese.
   - Use your hands or a spoon to mix them together until it forms a thick, dough-like mixture.
3. Shape into Balls:
   - Take small portions of the mixture and roll them into small balls using your hands. Aim for bite-sized truffles.
4. Melt the Chocolate:
   - Place the chocolate chips in a microwave-safe bowl.
   - Heat the chocolate in the microwave in 20-second intervals, stirring in between, until completely melted and smooth.
5. Coat the Truffles:
   - Use a fork or a toothpick to dip each Oreo ball into the melted chocolate, making sure it's fully coated.
   - Place the coated truffles on a parchment-lined tray.
6. Decorate (Optional):
   - If you want to add sprinkles, do it quickly before the chocolate hardens.
7. Chill:
   - Put the tray of truffles into the refrigerator for about 15-20 minutes to allow the chocolate to set.
8. Serve and Enjoy:
   - Once the chocolate is firm, your delicious No-Bake Oreo Truffles are ready to eat! They're great for parties or as a sweet treat.

Easy Fruit Pizza

Serves: 8 slices   **Prep time:** 15 min   **Cook time:** 12-15 min

INGREDIENTS

- 1 pre-made sugar cookie dough (or homemade if preferred)
- 1 package (8 ounces) cream cheese, softened
- 1/4 cup powdered sugar
- 1 teaspoon vanilla extract
- Assorted fruits (like strawberries, kiwi, blueberries, grapes, etc.)
- 1/4 cup apricot preserves or jelly (optional, for glaze)

DIRECTIONS

1. Preheat the oven to the temperature recommended on the sugar cookie dough package.
2. Roll out the sugar cookie dough onto a pizza pan or baking sheet lined with parchment paper. Press it down evenly to create the pizza crust.
3. Bake the cookie crust in the preheated oven according to the package instructions, usually for 12-15 minutes or until it turns golden brown.
4. Once done, remove it from the oven and let it cool completely.
5. In a mixing bowl, blend together the softened cream cheese, powdered sugar, and vanilla extract until smooth and creamy.
6. Once the cookie crust has cooled, spread the cream cheese mixture evenly over the crust, leaving a little space around the edges.
7. Wash and slice the fruits into small pieces or slices.
8. Arrange the assorted fruits on top of the cream cheese layer in any pattern you like. Get creative!
9. If you'd like a shiny finish, heat the apricot preserves or jelly in the microwave for about 20 seconds until it's slightly runny. Then lightly brush it over the fruit toppings.
10. For the best taste, refrigerate the fruit pizza for about 30 minutes before slicing.
11. Once chilled, cut it into slices and serve!

Chocolate-Dipped Pretzel Rods

Serves: 12-15 rods   Prep time: 15 min   Cook time: 5 min

INGREDIENTS

Pretzel rods

1 cup chocolate chips (milk, dark, or white)

Assorted toppings (sprinkles, crushed nuts, mini chocolate chips, etc.)

Wax paper or parchment paper

DIRECTIONS

1. **Prepare Toppings:**
   - Pour assorted toppings into separate bowls or plates.
2. **Melt the Chocolate:**
   - In a microwave-safe bowl, heat the chocolate chips in 30-second intervals, stirring in between, until melted and smooth. Be careful not to overheat the chocolate.
3. **Dip the Pretzel Rods:**
   - Dip each pretzel rod into the melted chocolate, covering about 2/3 of the rod. Let the excess chocolate drip off.
4. **Add Toppings:**
   - While the chocolate is still wet, roll the chocolate-coated pretzel rod in the assorted toppings. You can use sprinkles, crushed nuts, mini chocolate chips, or any other toppings you prefer.
5. **Set on Wax Paper:**
   - Place the decorated pretzel rods on wax paper or parchment paper to allow the chocolate to set.
6. **Optional Chill:**
   - If you want the chocolate to harden quickly, place the pretzel rods in the refrigerator for about 10-15 minutes.
7. **Serve and Enjoy:**
   - Once the chocolate has set, your chocolate-dipped pretzel rods are ready to be enjoyed!

Banana Sushi

Serves: 6-8 pieces   **Prep time: 10 min**   **Cook time: 0 min**

INGREDIENTS

1 ripe banana

Peanut butter or almond butter

Tortilla or flatbread

Honey or agave syrup (optional)

Toppings (such as shredded coconut, chocolate chips, chopped nuts, or sprinkles)

Plastic wrap (optional)

DIRECTIONS

1. Peel the banana and cut it into two or three sections for easier handling.
2. Lay the tortilla or flatbread on a clean surface.
3. Spread a layer of peanut butter or almond butter over the tortilla, covering it entirely. Leave a small margin around the edges.
4. Place the banana sections along one edge of the tortilla.
5. If desired, drizzle a little honey or agave syrup over the banana for added sweetness.
6. Carefully roll the tortilla around the banana sections, starting from the edge where the banana is placed. Roll it up tightly to create a sushi roll.
7. Use a sharp knife to slice the rolled tortilla into sushi-like pieces, each about an inch wide.
8. For a sushi-like appearance, you can wrap each slice with plastic wrap and gently shape them into a more cylindrical form. This step is optional but adds to the sushi presentation.
9. Sprinkle the tops of the banana sushi with shredded coconut, chocolate chips, chopped nuts, or colorful sprinkles. Get creative with the toppings!
10. Arrange the Banana Sushi pieces on a plate and enjoy this delightful treat!

Apple Nachos

Serves: 2-4   Prep time: 10 min   Cook time: 0 min

INGREDIENTS

2-3 apples (any variety)

1/4 cup peanut butter or almond butter

1/4 cup chocolate chips

1/4 cup shredded coconut

1/4 cup chopped nuts (optional)

1/4 cup dried cranberries or raisins (optional)

1 tablespoon honey or agave syrup (optional)

DIRECTIONS

1. Wash the apples thoroughly, then core and slice them into thin rounds or wedges. Arrange them in a single layer on a large serving plate or tray.
2. Warm the peanut butter or almond butter slightly in the microwave for easier drizzling.
3. Drizzle the nut butter evenly over the apple slices.
4. Sprinkle the chocolate chips, shredded coconut, chopped nuts (if using), and dried cranberries or raisins (if using) over the apple slices.
5. If desired, drizzle a bit of honey or agave syrup over the topped apples for extra sweetness.
6. Serve the Apple Nachos immediately and enjoy this delicious and healthy dessert!

Frozen Yogurt Bark

Serves: 4-6   Prep time: 10 min   Freeze time: 2-3 hrs

INGREDIENTS

2 cups Greek yogurt (any flavor)

2 tablespoons honey or maple syrup

1/2 cup mixed berries (strawberries, blueberries, raspberries)

1/4 cup granola or crushed graham crackers (optional)

2 tablespoons chocolate chips (optional)

DIRECTIONS

1. Prepare the Yogurt Mixture:
   - In a mixing bowl, combine the Greek yogurt and honey or maple syrup. Mix well until it's thoroughly combined.
2. Line a Tray:
   - Line a baking tray or a flat dish with parchment paper.
3. Spread the Yogurt:
   - Spread the yogurt mixture evenly onto the parchment paper, creating a smooth layer about 1/4 to 1/2 inch thick.
4. Add Toppings:
   - Sprinkle the mixed berries over the yogurt. You can also add granola or crushed graham crackers for extra texture and chocolate chips for a touch of sweetness.
5. Freeze the Bark:
   - Place the tray in the freezer and let the yogurt bark freeze for about 2-3 hours, or until it's completely firm.
6. Break into Pieces:
   - Once frozen, remove the bark from the freezer and break it into pieces using your hands or a knife.
7. Serve and Enjoy:
   - Serve the Frozen Yogurt Bark immediately as a delightful, cool treat for kids to enjoy!

Peanut Butter Energy Bites

Serves: 12-15 bites   Prep time: 15 min   Chill time: 30 min

INGREDIENTS

1 cup old-fashioned oats

1/2 cup peanut butter (or any nut or seed butter)

1/4 cup honey or maple syrup

1/4 cup mini chocolate chips (optional)

1/4 cup shredded coconut (optional)

1 teaspoon vanilla extract

DIRECTIONS

1. In a mixing bowl, combine the old-fashioned oats, peanut butter, honey or maple syrup, chocolate chips (if using), shredded coconut (if using), and vanilla extract. Mix until all ingredients are well combined.
2. Place the mixture in the refrigerator for about 10-15 minutes. Chilling it will make it easier to roll into balls.
3. Once chilled, take small portions of the mixture and roll them between your palms to form small, bite-sized balls. Aim for about 1-inch diameter balls.
4. Place the Peanut Butter Energy Bites on a plate or tray lined with parchment paper. Let them set in the refrigerator for an additional 15-20 minutes to firm up.
5. Once set, the Energy Bites are ready to enjoy! These can be stored in an airtight container in the refrigerator for up to a week.

Jelly Bean Bark

Serves: 8-10   Prep time: 10 min   Cook time: 10 min

INGREDIENTS

112 ounces (about 2 cups) white chocolate chips or candy melts

1 cup colorful jelly beans

Sprinkles (optional)

Parchment paper

DIRECTIONS

1. Line a baking sheet with parchment paper. Make sure it fits in your freezer or refrigerator.
2. In a microwave-safe bowl, melt the white chocolate chips or candy melts in 30-second intervals, stirring between each interval until smooth. Kids, be careful as the bowl might get hot!
3. Once the chocolate is melted, pour it onto the parchment paper-lined baking sheet. Use a spatula to spread it evenly into a rectangle about 1/4 inch thick.
4. Sprinkle the colorful jelly beans over the melted chocolate while it's still warm. This is the fun part—kids can create patterns or just scatter them around!
5. If you're using sprinkles, now's the time to add them! Sprinkle them over the jelly beans before the chocolate starts to set.
6. Place the baking sheet in the freezer or refrigerator for about 10 minutes or until the chocolate hardens completely.
7. Once the chocolate is firm, remove the baking sheet from the freezer or refrigerator. Let the bark sit for a minute or two to slightly soften, making it easier to break.
8. Kids, use your hands or a blunt knife to break the bark into fun, irregular pieces.
9. Your rainbow jelly bean bark is ready to enjoy! Store any leftovers in an airtight container in the refrigerator.

Mini Cheesecake Cups

Serves: 6   Prep time: 15 min   Cook time: 15-20 min

INGREDIENTS

12 Oreo cookies

8 ounces cream cheese, softened

1/4 cup granulated sugar

1 teaspoon vanilla extract

1 egg

Whipped cream (optional)

Fresh berries or fruit topping (optional)

DIRECTIONS

1. Preheat your oven to 325°F (160°C).
2. Place paper liners in a cupcake/muffin tray. This will make it easier to remove the mini cheesecakes later.
3. Place an Oreo cookie in the bottom of each paper liner. Kids, this will be the base of your mini cheesecakes.
4. In a mixing bowl, beat the softened cream cheese until smooth and creamy. Add in the sugar and vanilla extract. Mix until well combined.
5. Crack the egg into the cream cheese mixture. Mix until the batter is smooth. Kids, crack the egg into a separate bowl first to avoid any shell pieces!
6. Spoon the cheesecake batter over the Oreo cookies in the cupcake liners, filling each about 2/3 full.
7. Place the cupcake tray in the preheated oven and bake for 15-20 minutes or until the cheesecake is set but slightly jiggly in the center.
8. Once baked, remove the tray from the oven and let the mini cheesecakes cool in the tray for about 15 minutes. Then, transfer them to the refrigerator to chill for at least 1 hour or until completely cooled.
9. Kids, get creative! Before serving, add a dollop of whipped cream on top of each mini cheesecake and decorate with fresh berries or your favorite fruit topping.

Ice Cream Sandwiches

Serves: 6   Prep time: 10 min   Cook time: 30 min

INGREDIENTS

1 package of chocolate chip cookies (store-bought or homemade)

1 pint of your favorite ice cream flavor

Toppings (sprinkles, mini chocolate chips, crushed nuts, etc.)

DIRECTIONS

1. **Prepare the Cookies:**
    - If you're using homemade cookies, bake them according to the recipe instructions and let them cool completely. If using store-bought cookies, they're ready to go!
2. **Softening the Ice Cream:**
    - Take the ice cream out of the freezer and let it sit at room temperature for a few minutes to soften slightly. This will make it easier to work with.
3. **Assemble the Sandwiches:**
    - Pair up the cookies to create the sandwich base. Lay half of them, flat side up, on a baking sheet or a large plate.
4. **Add the Ice Cream:**
    - Using a spoon or an ice cream scoop, place a scoop of softened ice cream onto the flat side of each cookie on the baking sheet.
5. **Create the Sandwiches:**
    - Gently press the remaining cookies (flat side down) onto the ice cream scoops to create the sandwiches. Kids, press firmly but be gentle not to break the cookies!
6. **Add Toppings (Optional):**
    - Roll the edges of the ice cream sandwiches in your favorite toppings like sprinkles, mini chocolate chips, crushed nuts, or anything else you fancy! Get creative and have fun with this step.
7. **Freeze the Sandwiches:**
    - Place the assembled ice cream sandwiches in the freezer for at least 20-30 minutes to allow them to firm up.
8. **Serve and Enjoy:**
    - Once they're firm, your DIY ice cream sandwiches are ready to eat! Take them out of the freezer and enjoy these delicious treats.

Fruity Frozen Popsicles

Serves: 6-8   Prep time: 15 min   Freeze time: 4-6 hrs

INGREDIENTS

Assorted fruits (such as strawberries, blueberries, kiwi, pineapple, mango, etc.)

Fruit juice or coconut water

Popsicle molds

Popsicle sticks or plastic spoons

DIRECTIONS

1. Wash and chop the fruits into small, bite-sized pieces. Kids, this is a great chance to practice your knife skills with adult supervision!
2. Arrange the chopped fruits into the popsicle molds, mixing and matching different fruits in each mold to create colorful layers. Fill them about 3/4 of the way with the fruits.
3. Pour fruit juice or coconut water into the molds, filling them to the top. The liquid will fill the spaces between the fruit chunks. Leave a small gap at the top to allow for expansion during freezing.
4. Place the lids on the popsicle molds, if they have them, and then insert the popsicle sticks or plastic spoons into the center of each mold. Make sure they're straight and centered.
5. Carefully place the filled popsicle molds in the freezer and let them freeze for at least 4-6 hours or until completely solid.
6. Once the popsicles are frozen solid, take the molds out of the freezer. To remove the popsicles, run the mold under warm water for a few seconds to loosen them, then gently pull on the sticks to release the popsicles.
7. Your vibrant rainbow fruit popsicles are ready to enjoy! Share them with friends or enjoy them on a hot day as a refreshing treat.

Caramel Popcorn

Serves: 4-6   Prep time: 10 min   Cook time: 1 hr

INGREDIENTS

½ cup popcorn kernels

1 cup brown sugar

¼ cup unsalted butter

¼ cup light corn syrup

¼ teaspoon salt

¼ teaspoon baking soda

1 teaspoon vanilla extract

DIRECTIONS

1. Prepare the popcorn kernels using your preferred method (microwave, stovetop, or air popper). Make sure to remove any unpopped kernels.
2. Preheat your oven to 250°F (120°C) and line a large baking sheet with parchment paper or a silicone baking mat.
3. In a saucepan over medium heat, melt the butter. Add the brown sugar, corn syrup, and salt. Stir well until the mixture starts to boil.
4. Let the caramel boil without stirring for about 4-5 minutes. It should turn a golden brown color. Kids, be careful as the caramel will be very hot!
5. Remove the saucepan from the heat. Quickly stir in the baking soda and vanilla extract. The mixture will bubble up—this is normal.
6. Place the popped popcorn in a large mixing bowl. Pour the hot caramel sauce over the popcorn. Use a spatula or wooden spoon to gently toss and coat the popcorn evenly with the caramel.
7. Spread the coated popcorn onto the prepared baking sheet in an even layer.
8. Bake the caramel-coated popcorn in the preheated oven for about 45 minutes, stirring every 15 minutes to ensure even coating and prevent burning.
9. Once baked, remove the caramel popcorn from the oven and let it cool completely on the baking sheet. As it cools, the caramel will harden, creating crunchy caramel popcorn clusters.
10. Break the caramel popcorn into smaller clusters and serve it in bowls or store it in an airtight container for later munching.

Colorful Yogurt Parfait

Serves: 4   Prep time: 10 min   Cook time: 0 min

INGREDIENTS

2 cups Greek yogurt (vanilla or plain)

1 cup granola

1 cup mixed fresh fruits (strawberries, blueberries, bananas, etc.)

Honey or maple syrup (optional)

Sprinkles or shredded coconut (optional)

4 small clear glasses or jars

DIRECTIONS

1. Wash and chop the fresh fruits into small pieces. Kids, this is a chance to get creative with different fruit combinations!
2. Take the clear glasses or jars and begin assembling the parfait. Start by adding a spoonful of Greek yogurt as the first layer at the bottom of each glass.
3. Sprinkle a layer of granola over the yogurt in each glass. Then, add a layer of mixed fresh fruits on top of the granola. Repeat these layers until the glasses are almost full.
4. If desired, drizzle a bit of honey or maple syrup over the fruit layer to add extra sweetness. Kids, use a spoon to do this and be careful not to add too much!
5. Finish off the parfait by adding another dollop of Greek yogurt on top of the fruit layer in each glass.
6. For a playful touch, sprinkle some colorful sprinkles or shredded coconut on top of the yogurt layer. This step adds a fun element to the parfaits!
7. Your yogurt parfaits are ready to eat! Serve them immediately for a delightful treat or chill them in the refrigerator for a little while if you prefer them slightly chilled.

Graham Cracker Houses

Serves: Several   Prep time: 30 min   Cook time: 0 min

INGREDIENTS

Graham crackers (rectangular-shaped)
Royal icing or frosting
Assorted candies (gumdrops, mini marshmallows, M&M's, pretzels, etc.)
Small candies or sprinkles for decorating
Plastic knives or small spatulas
Plates or trays for assembling

DIRECTIONS

1. If using royal icing, prepare it according to the recipe or use store-bought frosting for easier preparation.
2. Place a graham cracker on a plate or tray. Use a generous amount of icing/frosting to "glue" another graham cracker upright to the first one to create the walls of the house. Hold them together for a minute to let the icing set.
3. Apply icing along the top edges of the walls and carefully place another graham cracker on top to form the roof of the house. Hold it in place for a moment to allow the icing to secure it.
4. Now comes the fun part! Use the icing as glue to attach assorted candies and decorations to the graham cracker house. Kids can get creative and design their houses with gumdrops as windows, mini marshmallows as snow, pretzels as fences, and more!
5. Allow the decorated houses to sit for a little while to let the icing dry and set completely. This will help the candies stay in place.
6. For added decoration, use smaller candies or sprinkles to create paths, gardens, or any other details around the houses.
7. Once the icing has set and the decorations are secured, kids can proudly display their graham cracker houses as edible decorations or enjoy them as a fun and tasty treat!

Chocolate Banana Bites

Serves: 12-15 bites   Prep time: 15 min   Cook time: 30 min

INGREDIENTS

2-3 ripe bananas

1 cup chocolate chips (dark, milk, or white chocolate)

Toppings (sprinkles, chopped nuts, shredded coconut, etc.)

Wooden popsicle sticks or toothpicks

DIRECTIONS

1. Peel the bananas and cut them into 1-inch chunks. Kids, make sure to use a blunt knife or ask an adult for help with cutting.
2. Insert a wooden popsicle stick or a toothpick into the center of each banana chunk. This will serve as the handle for dipping the bananas into chocolate.
3. Place the chocolate chips in a microwave-safe bowl. Microwave in 30-second intervals, stirring in between, until the chocolate is completely melted and smooth. Kids, be careful as the bowl might get hot!
4. Hold a banana chunk by the stick and dip it into the melted chocolate, coating it entirely. Use a spoon or spatula to help coat the banana evenly if needed.
5. Before the chocolate sets, sprinkle or roll the chocolate-coated banana in your choice of toppings, such as sprinkles, chopped nuts, or shredded coconut. Kids, have fun experimenting with different toppings!
6. Lay the chocolate-covered banana bites on a parchment-lined tray or plate. Place them in the refrigerator for about 15-20 minutes to allow the chocolate to set.
7. Once the chocolate is firm, your chocolate banana bites are ready to enjoy! Kids, grab them by the sticks and indulge in these tasty treats.

Marshmallow Rice Krispies

Serves: 12-16 squares   Prep time: 10 min   Cook time: 10 min

INGREDIENTS

3 tablespoons unsalted butter

4 cups mini marshmallows (or about 40 regular-sized marshmallows)

6 cups Rice Krispies cereal

DIRECTIONS

1. Grease a 9x13-inch baking dish with butter or line it with parchment paper. This will prevent the treats from sticking to the pan.
2. In a large saucepan, melt the butter over low heat. Once the butter is melted, add the marshmallows and stir continuously until they completely melt and combine with the butter. Kids, be careful with the hot pan!
3. Remove the saucepan from the heat. Pour in the Rice Krispies cereal and mix well until all the cereal is coated with the melted marshmallow mixture. Use a spatula or wooden spoon to combine.
4. Transfer the mixture into the prepared baking dish. Use a buttered spatula or your hands (lightly coated with butter or cooking spray to prevent sticking) to press the mixture firmly and evenly into the pan.
5. Allow the Rice Krispies treats to cool and set at room temperature for about 30 minutes to 1 hour. This will make them easier to cut into squares.
6. Once the treats have cooled and set, use a buttered knife to cut them into squares. Kids, get creative with the shapes if you like, but make sure an adult helps with cutting!
7. Your homemade marshmallow Rice Krispies treats are ready to be enjoyed! Serve them as a delicious dessert or snack.

Fruit Sorbet

Serves: 4-6   Prep time: 5 min   Cook time: 10 min

INGREDIENTS

3 cups frozen fruit (such as berries, mango, pineapple, or a combination)

1/4 cup honey or maple syrup (optional, for added sweetness)

1-2 tablespoons lemon juice (optional, for a tangy flavor)

1/4 cup water (if needed to help with blending)

DIRECTIONS

1. Ensure your chosen fruits are frozen. If they aren't frozen yet, place them in the freezer for a few hours or overnight until solid.
2. Place the frozen fruit in a food processor or blender. If using tougher fruits like mango or pineapple, you might need to let them sit for a few minutes to slightly thaw for easier blending.
3. Add honey, maple syrup, or any sweetener of your choice to the fruit in the blender. If you prefer a tangy flavor, squeeze in lemon juice. For smoother blending, add a splash of water if needed.
4. Blend the mixture until it becomes a smooth, creamy consistency. You may need to pause and scrape down the sides of the blender a few times to ensure everything is well mixed.
5. Taste the sorbet mixture and adjust the sweetness or tanginess by adding more sweetener or lemon juice if desired.
6. Pour the blended fruit sorbet mixture into a freezer-safe container or loaf pan. Smooth out the top with a spatula.
7. Cover the container with a lid or plastic wrap and place it in the freezer. Let the sorbet freeze for at least 4-6 hours or until it's firm.
8. Once the sorbet is fully frozen, use an ice cream scoop or spoon to scoop it into bowls or cones. Enjoy this refreshing and fruity treat!

Muddy Buddies

Serves: 8-10   Prep time: 15 min   Cook time: 15 min

INGREDIENTS

9 cups Chex cereal (rice, corn, or wheat)

1 cup chocolate chips (semi-sweet or milk chocolate)

1/2 cup peanut butter

1/4 cup unsalted butter

1 teaspoon vanilla extract

1 1/2 cups powdered sugar

DIRECTIONS

1. **Measure Chex Cereal:**
   - Place the Chex cereal in a large mixing bowl. Set it aside for later.
2. **Melt Chocolate, Peanut Butter, and Butter:**
   - In a microwave-safe bowl, combine the chocolate chips, peanut butter, and unsalted butter. Microwave in 30-second intervals, stirring between each, until the mixture is smooth and fully melted. Kids, be careful as the bowl might get hot!
3. **Add Vanilla Extract:**
   - Stir in the vanilla extract into the melted chocolate mixture until it's well combined.
4. **Coat the Cereal:**
   - Pour the melted chocolate mixture over the Chex cereal in the mixing bowl. Gently fold and stir until all the cereal is evenly coated with the chocolate mixture.
5. **Coat with Powdered Sugar:**
   - Sprinkle half of the powdered sugar over the chocolate-coated cereal and gently stir to coat. Then add the remaining powdered sugar and continue to mix until all the cereal pieces are covered with the powdered sugar coating.
6. **Let It Set:**
   - Spread the coated cereal out onto a baking sheet or a large tray lined with parchment paper in a single layer. Let it sit for a few minutes to allow the chocolate to set.
7. **Serve or Store:**
   - Once the muddy buddies have set, they're ready to be served! Enjoy them as a sweet snack. Store any leftovers in an airtight container at room temperature.

Chocolate-Covered Strawberries

Serves: ~12 strawberries   **Prep time:** 15 min   **Cook time:** 30 min

INGREDIENTS

1 pound fresh strawberries

6 ounces semi-sweet chocolate chips or chocolate melting wafers

Optional toppings (sprinkles, chopped nuts, shredded coconut)

DIRECTIONS

1. Rinse the strawberries under cold water and pat them dry thoroughly with paper towels. Make sure they are completely dry as moisture can prevent the chocolate from sticking.
2. Place the chocolate chips or melting wafers in a microwave-safe bowl. Microwave in 30-second intervals, stirring each time until the chocolate is completely melted and smooth. Be careful not to overheat the chocolate.
3. Line a baking sheet or a large plate with parchment paper. This will prevent the chocolate-covered strawberries from sticking to the surface.
4. Hold a strawberry by the stem and dip it into the melted chocolate, covering it about two-thirds of the way. Rotate and twist the strawberry as you lift it out to allow any excess chocolate to drip back into the bowl.
5. If you're using toppings like sprinkles, chopped nuts, or shredded coconut, sprinkle them over the chocolate-covered part of the strawberry before the chocolate starts to set.
6. Set the chocolate-covered strawberries onto the parchment paper-lined tray or plate, spacing them slightly apart from each other.
7. Once all the strawberries are coated, place the tray in the refrigerator for about 15-20 minutes or until the chocolate sets and hardens.
8. Once the chocolate has hardened, your chocolate-covered strawberries are ready to be enjoyed! Serve them as a delicious and elegant treat.

Cinnamon Sugar Tortilla Crisps

Serves: 4-6   Prep time: 5 min   Cook time: 10-12 min

INGREDIENTS

4-6 flour tortillas (6-8 inches in diameter)

2 tablespoons unsalted butter, melted

1/4 cup granulated sugar

1 teaspoon ground cinnamon

DIRECTIONS

1. Preheat your oven to 350°F (175°C).
2. Brush both sides of each flour tortilla with melted butter using a pastry brush or a spoon. Kids, make sure to cover them evenly.
3. In a small bowl, mix together the granulated sugar and ground cinnamon until well combined.
4. Sprinkle the cinnamon sugar mixture generously over both sides of each buttered tortilla. Make sure to coat them evenly.
5. Stack the tortillas on top of each other and use a pizza cutter or a knife to cut them into triangles or desired shapes. Kids, get creative with shapes!
6. Place the cinnamon sugar-coated tortilla triangles in a single layer on baking sheets lined with parchment paper or aluminum foil.
7. Bake in the preheated oven for 10-12 minutes or until the tortilla crisps are golden brown and crispy. Keep an eye on them to prevent burning.
8. Remove the baking sheets from the oven and let the tortilla crisps cool for a few minutes. They will continue to crisp up as they cool down.
9. Your homemade cinnamon sugar tortilla crisps are ready to be enjoyed! Serve them as a tasty snack or a crunchy dessert.

Mini Fruit Tarts

Serves: 6-12 tarts   Prep time: 15 min   Cook time: 20 min

INGREDIENTS

1 package (about 12) pre-made mini tart shells (store-bought or homemade)

1/2 cup whipped cream or pastry cream (store-bought or homemade)

Assorted fresh fruits (strawberries, blueberries, kiwi, raspberries, etc.)

2 tablespoons fruit jelly or apricot preserves (optional, for glaze)

Fresh mint leaves (optional, for garnish)

DIRECTIONS

1. Prepare the Tart Shells:
   - If using store-bought tart shells, they're typically pre-baked. If using homemade, bake according to the recipe instructions and let them cool completely before starting.
2. Fill with Whipped Cream or Pastry Cream:
   - Spoon a dollop of whipped cream or pastry cream into each mini tart shell. Kids, you can use a spoon or a piping bag to fill them neatly.
3. Slice the Fresh Fruits:
   - Wash and slice the fresh fruits into small pieces. Kids, remember to get adult help when using knives!
4. Decorate with Fresh Fruits:
   - Arrange the sliced fruits on top of the whipped cream or pastry cream in the tart shells. Get creative with different fruit combinations or make colorful patterns!
5. Optional Glaze (For Shine):
   - Heat the fruit jelly or apricot preserves in the microwave for a few seconds until it's runny. Brush a thin layer over the arranged fruits to give them a glossy finish. Kids, be careful as the jelly might be hot!
6. Garnish with Mint Leaves (Optional):
   - If desired, add a small mint leaf or two on top of the fruits for a decorative touch.
7. Chill or Serve Immediately:
   - Chill the mini fruit tarts in the refrigerator for about 10-15 minutes to let them set, or they can be served immediately.
8. Serve and Enjoy:
   - Your mini fruit tarts are ready to be enjoyed! Serve them as a delightful dessert or sweet snack.

Candy-Coated Pretzel Rods

Serves: 12-16 rods   **Prep time:** 15 min   **Cook time:** 30 min

INGREDIENTS

12-16 pretzel rods

1 cup candy melts or chocolate chips (assorted colors or flavors)

Assorted toppings (sprinkles, crushed nuts, mini candies)

DIRECTIONS

1. Prepare Toppings:
   - If using toppings like sprinkles, crushed nuts, or mini candies, place each topping in separate bowls or shallow dishes. Kids, arrange them in a way that's easy to access for decorating.
2. Melt the Candy Coating:
   - Place each type of candy melts or chocolate chips in separate microwave-safe bowls. Microwave them in 30-second intervals, stirring in between until they are fully melted and smooth. Be careful not to overheat.
3. Coat the Pretzel Rods:
   - Dip each pretzel rod into the melted candy coating, covering about two-thirds of the rod. Rotate and twist the rod as you lift it out to allow any excess coating to drip back into the bowl.
4. Decorate with Toppings:
   - While the candy coating is still wet, sprinkle or roll the coated parts of the pretzel rods into the assorted toppings. Kids, get creative and make colorful and textured designs!
5. Place on a Tray to Set:
   - Lay the decorated pretzel rods on a parchment-lined baking sheet or a tray in a single layer, making sure they're not touching each other.
6. Let Them Set:
   - Allow the candy-coated pretzel rods to set and harden. You can place them in the refrigerator for about 15-20 minutes to speed up the setting process.
7. Serve or Store:
   - Once the candy coating has completely set, your candy-coated pretzel rods are ready to be enjoyed! Serve them as a fun and tasty treat. Store any leftovers in an airtight container at room temperature.

Frozen Banana Pops

Serves: 4-8   Prep time: 15 min   Cook time: 1 hr 15 min

INGREDIENTS

4 ripe bananas
1 cup chocolate chips (semi-sweet or milk chocolate)
2 tablespoons coconut oil or vegetable oil
Assorted toppings (sprinkles, chopped nuts, shredded coconut)
Wooden popsicle sticks or skewers

DIRECTIONS

1. Peel the bananas and cut them in half crosswise. Insert a wooden popsicle stick or skewer into the cut end of each banana half. Place them on a parchment-lined tray or plate.
2. Place the bananas in the freezer for about 1 hour or until they are firm. This will make them easier to dip into the chocolate.
3. In a microwave-safe bowl, combine the chocolate chips and coconut oil. Microwave in 30-second intervals, stirring each time until the chocolate is completely melted and smooth.
4. Remove the bananas from the freezer. Dip each banana into the melted chocolate, coating it entirely. Rotate and twist the banana as you lift it out to allow any excess chocolate to drip back into the bowl.
5. While the chocolate is still wet, sprinkle the coated bananas with assorted toppings like sprinkles, chopped nuts, or shredded coconut. Kids, get creative with different toppings!
6. Lay the chocolate-coated bananas on the parchment-lined tray or plate, making sure they're not touching each other.
7. Place the tray back into the freezer and let the chocolate-covered bananas freeze until the chocolate is firm, usually for about 30-45 minutes.
8. Once the chocolate is set and the bananas are frozen, your frozen banana pops are ready to be enjoyed! Kids, take them out of the freezer and indulge in these tasty treats.

Berry Smoothie Bowls

Serves: 2   Prep time: 10 min   Cook time: 10 min

INGREDIENTS

2 ripe bananas, frozen

1 cup mixed berries (strawberries, blueberries, raspberries)

1/2 cup Greek yogurt

1/4 cup milk (any kind)

Toppings: Sliced fruits (bananas, strawberries, kiwi), granola, shredded coconut, chia seeds, honey

DIRECTIONS

1. Peel and slice the bananas before freezing them. Wash the mixed berries and pat them dry.
2. In a blender, combine the frozen bananas, mixed berries, Greek yogurt, and milk. Blend until smooth. Kids, be careful when using the blender!
3. Check the consistency of the smoothie. If it's too thick, add a little more milk and blend again until you reach a creamy, spoonable consistency.
4. Divide the blended smoothie mixture into serving bowls.
5. Let the kids get creative! Arrange sliced fruits, granola, shredded coconut, chia seeds, or any preferred toppings over the smoothie bowls. They can create patterns or designs with the toppings!
6. For a touch of sweetness, drizzle a bit of honey over the top of the smoothie bowls.
7. Your delicious and nutritious berry smoothie bowls are ready to be enjoyed! Kids, grab a spoon and dig into these colorful and healthy treats.

Conclusion

As we wrap up our flavorful journey through "Little Bakers, Big Flavors: Fun, Easy & Unique Desserts for Young Chefs," I hope these recipes have ignited a passion for baking within our young culinary enthusiasts. The kitchen is a canvas, and each dessert created is a masterpiece, a testament to creativity and skill.

Through these pages, our budding chefs have discovered the joy of crafting delightful treats, from simple cookies to elegant parfaits, learning not just the art of baking but also the value of patience, precision, and creativity. The kitchen has been their playground, a place where imagination flourishes and where they've embraced the joy of experimentation.

As this cookbook closes, let's celebrate the shared moments and laughter that came with measuring, mixing, and decorating. These experiences are more than just about desserts; they're about bonding, making memories, and fostering a love for culinary adventures. May these recipes continue to inspire our young chefs to explore, innovate, and share their delicious creations with loved ones, keeping the joy of baking alive in their hearts. Here's to many more sweet adventures in the kitchen!

Your feedback is greatly appreciated!

It's through your feedback, support and reviews that I'm able to create the best books possible and serve more people.

I would be extremely grateful if you could take just 60 seconds to kindly leave an honest review of the book on Amazon. Please share your feedback and thoughts for others to see.

To do so, simply find the book on Amazon's website (or wherever you purchased the book from) and locate the section to leave a review. Select a star rating and write a couple of sentences.

That's it! Thank you so much for your support.

Review this product

Share your thoughts with other customers

Write a customer review

References

- OpenAI. (2023). Conversations with ChatGPT. Retrieved [Dec 26, 2023], from https://www.openai.com/chatgpt/

References